1

My Darkest Hours

By Randy Wallace

www.writersblockpublishing.net

Written by Randy Wallace at rwrelationship@yahoo.com.
Facebook: Randy Wallace of Dallas, Texas.

Forward

Writing this book is something that I have been struggling with for years. I guess I was more ashamed and embarrassed of what people might think about me and what they would say. But after five years of thinking, "Should I or shouldn't I," I had a long talk with myself and My God. We both agreed to go ahead and write it.

This book is not like any of my others. This book talks about a time in my life that no one ever knew about, a time in my life that I never talked about with anyone, a time in my life when I thought about taking my own life: My Darkest Hours. My darkest hours were when I thought my life was just about to be over and God had turned His back on me. I lost or was losing everything I owned and for which I had worked so hard. This included a good job that paid me 45k a year with the best health benefits, a new home that I just bought, a new car, a credit score of 760 that took me years to build, a 401k that had over 15k in it, a checking and savings account that had a combined total of 13k in them, and five major credit cards. Two of the cards had a 10k credit limit and the other three had a 5k credit limit on them. I lived a life style that I enjoyed very much.

All these things, I lost except for my home - and only by filing for bankruptcy was I able to save that. I lost all these things, but not because I was foolish with my money or spending more money than I had. No, I lost all these things because of an accident I had on my job. It wasn't a serious, life-threatening, or hospital-staying type of accident. I never thought this accident would change my life forever. I never thought that one day, I would wake up and go to work to do a job that I done the same way every day for over six years to a man, who, 13 months after having this accident, lost my job, my health benefits, had to cash out my 401k, and close out my checking and savings account just to pay bills. I was a man who was afraid of driving his car because he didn't want to run into the repo man. I was a man who didn't want to go to the mailbox because he knew the only thing that was in the box was bills, late payment notices, final notices payment, termination notices, and foreclosure notices.

With all that going on in my life, I started self-medicating with drugs alcohol, Jack Daniel's and pain pills, Vicodin and Hydrocortisone. I got these pills illegally from a drug dealing friend of mines because I had no health insurance and no money to buy legal prescription medication. I was experiencing depression and chronic pain that kept me up all day and night. I would lie to myself that I took the alcohol and the pain pills to relieve the pain, but I knew in my heart that I took them to escape the reality of my situation.

One night, as I sat on the side of my bed with a bottle of Jack Daniel's in my left hand and my Glock 9 mm handgun in my right hand, I thought about ending my life.

"Why me?" I asked God. "God, why are you allowing these things to happen to me? What did I do that was so wrong?" What I didn't know was that this was just the start of a long journey that God had for my life - a journey that would change my life forever. This is my testimony about how in my darkest hour, God shined his loving light on me and brought me out of the darkest and the despair that had filled my life.

The Start of a New Life

The year was 2004. My 25 years of working as a General Manager for a large uniform company had come to an end. After taking a couple of years off from work just to rest, I was ready to go back to work. But Corporate America is not something in which I want to get back.

After looking through the want ads for months, I saw an ad for a pest control technician. The add said that no experience was needed and that they will train the employee. This would be something new for me. All of my adult life had been spent working in the retail and uniform industry, so I decided to give it a try. To my amazement, I really liked the pest control business. I had a company truck and was out of the office all day - something that I was used to doing at my old job. I really didn't want an office job or a job that kept me inside. That's not the kind of person I am.

I went to work as a residential technician. That meant that I did houses. It was January when I stated and I liked it. When the weather was bad or it was rainy, the customers would call in and reschedule or cancel their service for that day and I would get to go home earlier that day. What I didn't know was that come summer time, we worked long hours in the hot sun. That wasn't for me.

After working a couple of years, I transferred to the commercial side of the company. This side did restaurants, apartments, offices buildings, and other commercial properties. The bad thing about working commercial was that most of the time, my day would start at 1:00 a.m. This was because when you treat a restaurant kitchen, you have to be in and out before the cooks come in to prepare the food. Even though the restaurant didn't open until 10 -11:00 a.m., they had people to come in at 4 - 5:00 a.m. to start pepping food. Most of the time, I would start work 1:00 a.m. and work to 2 or 3:00 p.m. I didn't mind because the money was great. I never thought I could make 45k a year just by killing roaches. I did!

I liked my job and I was good at it. The best part was that I made my own hours. I worked as many hours as I wanted or as few hours as I wanted. Another the good thing about this job was that I never had to pay for breakfast, lunch, or dinner. The bad thing about this job was that I gain 30 lbs because I ate at every restaurant I treated for free! Another good thing about this job was that I didn't have to go into the offices except for once a week for a technician's meeting and to restock on chemicals. I only saw my supervisor once a week and that was one time too many for me.

After about two years as a technician, I was offered a supervisor position. I declined it. After over 25 years of managing people, the only person I wanted to supervise was myself.

Almost 50 Years Old and Buying My First Home

In 2007, I brought my first home. I had a good paying job and thought it was time for me to buy a home. All my life, I had lived in apartments, The one I was living in, I had lived in for 16 years. I was 49 years old and it was past time for me to own a home.

Getting my home was easy. I had good credit and I thought I was responsible and mature enough to own

8

my own home now that my lifestyle have change from being street smart to being responsible smart. I had no idea of the responsibility that came with the ownership of a home. Now I know the difference between paying rent and paying a mortgage - about $850.00 a month.

I went from paying $550.00 a month for rent to paying $1,300.00 a month for mortgage. I went from paying $45.00 a month for utilities in my apartment to a house light bill that in the summertime would be $200 - $300.00 just for lights. But that was easy. I was making good money and I was excited about having something I could call my own.

Now that I had my own home, all I needed was someone with whom to share it. I met that someone in 2005 and two years later, we moved into our first home. It was her first new home too. She had been married years ago, and they lived in her ex-husband's grandmother's old house in the country. She was just as excited as I was about having her own home.

We moved in during 2007, and the first thing I did when I moved in was get a dog, Goldie. I always wanted a dog. When I got my own home, and I finally had the three things that I always wanted - a home, a special woman to share it with, and a dog. A couple months later, we got another dog, Pirate. He was more her dog than mine. But like everything else in my life, nothing lasts forever.

A couple years later, Goldie ran away. A year later, my lady and I broke up and she moved out. But we remain friends to this day. She left and took some of the furniture. I kept the dog, Pirate, and the house.

2009: The Housing Market Crashed and It Landed on Me

The year was 2009. My lady and I had broken up and I needed to do something to help me with the household expenses. I went to my bank, Bank of America, to see if I could get a loan modification so I could lower my mortgage payments on my home. I was told that I could not get a home modification because I was not three months or more behind on my mortgage. The lady at Bank of America told me not to pay my mortgage for three months, come back in three months, and that Bank of America would then give me a loan modification.

I didn't understand why I had to be behind on my mortgage just to get a loan modification, but I was a new home owner. I been banking with Bank of America for over twenty years and I never had any problems with them. But my trust in Bank of America turned into the worst experience I ever had in my life. After filling out paperwork and sending it in, and re-sending the same document in over and over, I received a letter from Bank of America. They said they were foreclosing on my home for non-payment. I couldn't believe what I was reading! Bank of America was foreclosing on my home after I was told by one of their employees at their bank that I had to be three months behind on my mortgage before I could get a loan modification. Now that I was three months behind on my mortgage, Bank of America was going to foreclose on my home. I didn't understand.

To make matters worse, every time I called Bank of America to talk about the problem, I would talk to a different person. Those people were very rude and unprofessional. The employees at Bank of America gave me the impression that they didn't care about me or my problem. I found out a couple of years later that between 2009 – 2010, Bank of America had foreclosed or had taken over two million homes from people in one year. Some of them were in a loan modification. Shame on you, Bank of America.

In 2012, I was part of a government class action lawsuit against Bank of America that ended with Bank of America paying out hundreds of millions of dollars to homeowners who lost their homes to foreclosure. I got a whopping 1,300.00. Thank you, Bank of America.

Bankruptcy was My Only Choice

Now I didn't know what to do. I was about to lose my home and trying to talk to anyone at Bank of America to get help to resolve this problem was impossible. Now I was getting all these letters in the mail from bankruptcy attorneys and people telling me that they could stop the foreclosure on my home. I hated to go to the mailbox because there would be fifteen or twenty letters in my mail box every day. I didn't know anything about bankruptcy or how it worked, but I learned it was my only choice if I wanted to keep my home.

I made the choice to go and talk to a bankruptcy attorney. I was shocked to find out how bankruptcy worked. I could not file bankruptcy because I was not in debt or behind on my bills. I had a 760 credit score and five major credit cards that were all current and up to date. In order to file to save my home, I had to include my car that I was not behind on and any other thing for which I was paying. In short, I had to give up my good credit that I had worked for 30 years to establish just to

11

save my home. Thank you very much, Bank of America. So I did all of that and I was able to at least save my home. But my good credit was a thing of the past.

The Only Choice I Had

After talking to the bankruptcy attorney, I was driving home, thinking about the choice that I had to make. My choices were to file bankruptcy and save everything I worked so hard to build, or walk away from my new home for which I had prayed to God for years. I asked Him to bless me so I could keep some of the good credit and things that I had worked so hard to build.

After arriving at my home, I sat in my living for a couple of hours and thought about the choice I had to make. I made my decision. I got up from the sofa, went to the bar, and got a bottle of Jack Daniel's and five shot glasses. I went to the kitchen table and filled each shot glass with Jack Daniel's. Then I pulled out my wallet, got my credit cards, and laid one on top of each shot glass. I then went and got a pair of scissors. I sat at the table. I removed the credit card from on top of each shot glass. As I drank the Jack Daniel's that was in the glass, I would cut up the credit card that was on top of it.

For over 30 years, Jack Daniel's has always brought lots of joy to my life. But that day, no matter how much Jack Daniel's I drank, I could not feel any happiness - only the pain of losing everything that I had worked so hard to get.

The Fall that Changed My Life

March 17, 2011, 10:27 a.m. I will remember this day for the rest of my life. This is the day my life changed forever. Six years later, I still have nightmares about that day. I thank God that He allowed me to live through it.

The day started like any other day. I got up, went to work, and did the same things I did every day. I got a call that one of the buildings I treated had a bad smell coming from the air vents. People in the bank building thought something had died in the vents. I went to the bank. Before going in, I got my ladder from my truck and started my inspection of the air vent. I checked several sections of the bank's air vents, but couldn't find out where the odor was coming from. I moved my ladder around the bank and placed the ladder in the same way that I did all the other times, but something freaky happened this time.

As I was coming down my ladder, I felt it move. When it moved again, I knew something was terribly wrong. I felt the ladder starting to tilt over. I knew I had to get down and off. The next thing I knew, I was falling! I tried to jump off, but somehow my foot slipped and my left leg was caught in between the steps. As I was falling, I noticed I was falling in the direction of a large, glass window.

"Please, God, don't let me fall through that glass window," I asked God. At that moment, I felt something that I can't explain to this day. It felt like a gust of wind or that someone pushed me. It wasn't a hard push, just enough that when I hit the floor, I landed about three inches from the glass window. When I hit the floor, I landed on my right shoulder. My head bounced off the floor. I was in a daze after the fall and didn't know I had a concussion.

The bank manager ran over and asked me if I was alright. I could hear her, but I could not see her. My vision was blurred and I had a bad headache. I tried to move, but my left leg was caught in the steps of the ladder. I looked at my leg and it was pointed in the wrong direction. The pain coming from it was worse than the pain coming from my head. Just then, I heard the siren coming from the ambulance as it got closer. I must have blacked out for a moment, for the next thing I heard was one of the paramedics calling my name and telling me to try not to fall asleep. The paramedics managed to pull my left leg from between the ladder steps. They put an air cast on my leg and a neck brace on my neck. They lifted me onto a gurney and put me in the ambulance.

As the paramedics were working on me, I heard one of them say they he had talked to the bank manager. She told them that when she looked up and saw me falling, she thought I would fall through the glass window. He said that if I would have fallen three inches to the left, I would have gone through the glass window.

All Thanks and Praises to God

In the emergency room, I was in so much pain that I was thinking I was going to die. I thought I was paralyzed, as I couldn't feel my left leg. They took x-rays of my head, neck, left leg, back, and shoulder. By the grace of God, there were no broken bones. Still, the emergency room doctor wanted me to go get an MRI just to be sure because I was still in a lot of pain. He said I had some bad looking bruises. The doctor told me the fall could have been a lot worse. I could have easily damaged my neck and spine and have been paralyzed. He said that I had a concussion, but I would be all right and the headaches would stop in a couple of days. I never thought I would wake up go to work one day and have a fall like that. I did things the same things the same ways for six years without that problem.

Working through the Pain

After leaving the emergency room, I went home. Even though I was still in a lot of pain when I got home, the first thing I did was to fall to my good knee and thank God for bringing me through this accident. I went to see my personal doctor the next day. After he looked at the x-rays, he said he wanted me to take a couple of weeks off of work because I was still in a lot of pain. He told me going to work would do nothing but make my injuries worse. My doctor told me he wanted to do an MRI on my neck, back, left knee, and right shoulder to see if there were any muscles, nerve, or tissue damaged.

During the time I was off, my job kept calling me and asking me when was I coming back to work. They even sent a supervisor to my house to see if my injuries were as bad as I said they were. Even though I had a brace on my left leg and knee and my right arm was in a sling, they told me that if I didn't show up for work Monday, I would no longer have a job. It was Thursday evening when he came over. I showed him the letter I had from my doctor, stating that I need to have an MRI done before he would release me back to work. He called the offices and talked to the manager. The manager told him to tell me that if there was not anything broken, that I had to be back at work Monday or I would not have a job.

So Monday came and I went back to work with a knee brace on my left knee. I was still in a lot of pain, but I needed my job. After a few days, I started to have more pain in my right arm and shoulder to the point that it was getting hard to lift my arm or anything. So I made another appointment with my doctor to see what was wrong and why I was having so much pain in my shoulder.

No Help From My Job

I went to my doctor and told him what was happening with my shoulder. He said he would have to do an MRI to find out what was going on, as the x-ray didn't tell him what he needed to know. He asked me if I had health insurance on my job, and I said yes. He said that I would need to see an orthopedic specialist because I might have tissue damage that the x-rays don't show. He said that he would contact them and get it approved.

Later that week, he contacted me and said the insurance company told him that since I got hurt on the job, worker's comp would have to pay for the MRI. I was not covered for an on-the job-injury. The doctor told me to go to my job and tell them that I needed to have an MRI done on my right shoulder and left knee. I did and I got no help from my job. They didn't want to get worker's comp in void because they didn't want their insurance premiums to go up. My job told me to find a doctor and have him do the MRI. They would pay the bill with a company credit card.

Now by me being a General Manager for over twenty years and someone who had worked with worker's compensation on several different occasions, I knew this is not the way things worked. I had no choice, though. I was calling around and trying to find a doctor to do the MRI. For days, I called around. Everyone I talked to told me the same thing - that I had to be referred to an orthopedic specialist by my private doctor and I needed to have a worker's comp claim number. They told me that my job had to report any injuries or accident to worker's comp and worker's comp would issue me a number. I told them I knew that information, but my job kept telling me they would pay for the MRI with a company credit card. I was told to go back and talk to my job. I needed to get referred to worker's comp before I could see a doctor.

Now days had passed and I was in a great deal of pain with my right shoulder to the point I couldn't hardly use my right arm for anything. I could barely walk or stand on my left leg. I told my supervisor I was in too much pain to work and I needed to get worker's comp involved. I needed to get an MRI done on my shoulder to find out what was going on. I had to take off work because I couldn't use my right arm and I was right-handed. He told me to go to the office and talk to the office manager. I told him she knew what was going on and she keep telling me to find a doctor that would take a company credit card for payment. He told me if I took off work, I would lose my job. I told him that due to my on-the-job injuries, I was not able to do my job. I let him know that if he wanted to fire me, to go ahead - but I was going to get some help for my shoulder.

17

I left the job and called my insurance company to tell them what had happened with my injury. They said they wouldn't cover the whole cost of the MRI because it was an on-the-job injury. If my job had worker's compensation, they would pay for the cost of the MRI and anything else I needed.

At this point, I was out of options and losing the use of my right arm. The pain was unbearable, so I called an MRI clinic to find out how much the MRI would cost. I was willing to pay for it myself. They told me the total cost would be $3,200 dollars and I had to pay it at the time of the MRI. The lady also told me that since I my injury was an on-the-job injury, that I should file a claim with worker's compensation. I could do it myself without my job.

Taking Matters into My Own Hands

After about three weeks of calling around to doctors, I called worker's comp myself. I told them about the accident, how it happened, and the date it happened. I told them that it had been a month since my injury and that I still hadn't received any medical help. The company that I worked for kept telling me to call around and find a doctor that would take a company credit card. The lady at worker's compensation told me that's not how it worked. She asked me who I worked for and I told her. She checked and said the company did have worker's compensation insurance and they should have contact them the first day the accident happen so I could get some medical help. I told her that I had to take off work for about a month and that I was not getting paid. I was paying for my own doctor visits out of my own pocket because my health insurance wouldn't pay for the doctor visit because I was hurt on the job. She told me that the company I worked for had health insurance and they didn't pay for an on-the-job injury, which is the purpose for which worker's compensation is used.

Worker's Compensation to the Rescue! God is Good!

After my talk with the worker's comp lady, she got in touch with my job and got me the help I needed. My job was very upset with me for getting them involved, but I didn't care. I was finally going to get the help I needed.

After a week, worker's comp gave me the okay to get the MRI and it showed that I had a rotator cuff tear in my right shoulder and had to have surgery. A second MRI revealed that I had torn ACL in my left knee. In four years, that would lead me to have a total knee replacement. A third MRI revealed that I had three bulging discs in my neck.

Now that worker's comp stepped in, I got the surgery I needed for my shoulder. I did not get the money back that I paid out of pocket for doctor visits. At that point, I was getting a check every week for being off. Everything had worked out for the best in my life, or so I thought. But what I didn't know about the changes and challenges that was coming my way would test my Faith, Belief, and Trust in my God in ways I never expected.

Off Work; Out of a Job

After worker's comp got involved, everything worked out. They gave me the go ahead for my surgery. The doctor told me the surgery would be more complex than he thought because the MRI showed that the damage to my shoulder was severe. It would take long to heal. I would be off work for about a year. There was no guarantee that at my age, 52, I would be able to do that job again. My job as a pest control technical had a lot of heavy lifting. We lifted boxes well over a hundred pounds and moved furniture and kitchen appliances in restaurants.

The doctor said that I had lost a lot of my range in motion in my right arm . By doing a lot of heavy lifting, I could possibly re-injure it worse. I was off work for about a year. Even though worker's comp did pay me 70% of my salary, it was not like get paid 100% of your salary. Each month, I had to dip into my savings to make up for the lost income.

A year later, I was ready to get back to work. However, I could only do light duties - no heavy lifting. I contacted my job and told them that I was ready to come back to work, but that I could only do light lifting. My supervisor told me they did not have any light lifting and I could not work there anymore doing pest control.

No Job, No Health Insurance, No Money

After having the rotator cuff surgery, I lost the use of my right arm for a couple of months. Being right-handed, I couldn't do a lot of things for myself. After being off of work for a year due to my injuries, my job terminated me and I lost my health benefits. I was able to get pain medication through worker's comp, but the money had run out.

I now I had to live off my 401k and my checking

and savings money. After losing my job, I had to close out my 401k and use the money to help pay some bills, such as my mortgage, car note, food, and other things. Even though worker's comp had paid me 70% of my salary, I still had to make up for the other 30% on my own. Living alone with only one pay check coming was very hard.

As the months went by, so did the money. The worker's comp payment had run out. After about a year, my 401k money was gone. I was living off money that I had in my checking and savings account. A few month later, all the money was gone but the bills were still coming in. I had no idea how I was going to pay them.

I was suffering from the 3 D's: Depression, Desperation, and Despair. Then one day as I was going through some papers, I found one of my old check stubs from my job. As I looked at it, I saw that my job was taking out for long term disability insurance. So I called my job and got the number. Thank God I was covered! OH HAPPY DAY!! Now I had money coming and I could pay my bills. But the money could only pay my bills and my mortgage. I had to do without my pain medication.

Choosing Between Bills and Pain Medication

Now I had money coming, but it was only enough to pay my bills. I had to do without pain medication. I have had injuries before, but nothing like this. The pain in my neck, back, shoulder, and left leg and knee was unbearable I couldn't sleep I was up all night. I was only able to sleep two or three hour a night. The pain kept me up all night. Because of the damage to my

21

knee, I could hardly walk or stand for more than a short period of time. With no money for pain medication, I started to self-medicate with pain pills and other drugs that I was getting from a drug dealer friend of mine. I was also drinking alcohol all day, every day.

Now was having to deal with the chronic pain in my body, the bankruptcy and foreclosure on my home, and the loss of my health benefits and job. This went on for over a year.

All the time am asking myself, "God, why are you allowing this to happen to me? I wasn't a bad person. I never killed anyone. I always treated people nicely. I went to church - not every Sunday, but I went."

I was only able to drive to the grocery store or run a few errands at a time because it was too painful to get in and out of my car or walk for a long period of time. I have always lived alone. For the most part of my life, I loved it. At that point, I could barely get around in my own home and was wishing I had someone there to help me or just to talk to me.

Doing the drugs and the alcohol made it easier to deal with everything that was going on in my life. All day and night, I would sit and think about the life I had before my accident. I'd think about all the fun things I done and the trips I had taken. Now I could hardly walk and barely stand. I had no one here to talk to or help me around the house. I just kept doing the drugs and alcohol. Sometimes I wouldn't know if it was day or night outside or what day it was because I wouldn't even go outside or look out the window.

God, Help Me, Please: Through Deliverance or Death, I Don't Care

That was my cry every day and night. I thought about ending my life, but my Christian upbringing and my belief in God would not let me. I couldn't understand why the God I prayed to all my life would allow me to go through what I was going through. I didn't see any light at the end of the tunnel and I was not getting any better. The chronic pain and depression had taken over my life and it had become a way of life.

I would just set and think all day and night about my life and the way I had lived it. I was by no means a saint, but I wasn't a bad person. I didn't deserve anything like this. It's funny. It seems like when I was well, working, and able to move around, I never had enough time think about my life and the way I was living it. Suddenly, I had all this time in the world and all I could do is sit in the dark, in pain, and think where my life was going.

As a little boy, my mother always taught me and my siblings to pray, trust, have faith, and believe in the Lord. All my life, I had done that. But after over two years and my situation hadn't changed, well, I guessed that God was not listening to me anymore. At this point, I stopped praying for help and started praying for death by any means. Just to deliver me from the pain and depression I was going through.

Social Security Disability: Another Problem

The year is 2013 two years after my accident and nothing has changed maybe myself medication has increased but the chronic pain, depression and problem are still there.

One day I went to see my personal physician. As I was telling him about my problems, he suggest that I file for my Social Security Disability. Then I would be able to get the help I needed. He said he would sign the paper, because in his opinion, I was not able to work on any job.

So I decided to fill for my Social Security Disability. After all, in 2009, I received a letter in the mail from them saying that I had earned enough credit that if I became disabled, I would qualify to get my Social Security Disability Benefits. I called them and they sent me the papers. I filled them out and even went to see their doctor. Six months later, a received a letter saying they had denied me. Well, that almost pushed me over the edge. A bullet to the head was starting to look better and better.

A Four Year Review of My Life

That night, I sat and reviewed my life over the past four years. In 2010, I went to Bank of America to get a loan modification to lower my mortgage payments and they tried to foreclose on my home. I had to file bankruptcy to save my home. I had to give up a good 760 credit score that I had worked so hard to build.

In 2011, I had fallen due to an accident that left me unable to work, and left me with injuries to my right shoulder, left leg, knee, back, and neck. As a result of these injuries, I had to have two rotator cuff surgeries to fix the damage to my right shoulder. I later found out after the second surgery that they had found nerve damage in my right shoulder that would limit the use of my right arm. It would eventually cause me to develop carpal tunnel in my right hand. As a result of the fall, I had a torn ACL in my left knee and had to wear a knee brace just to walk or stand. It was almost impossible to walk, drive, or get in and out of my car. As a result of a concussion from my head hitting the floor after the fall, I now had very serious migraines and my eyes were very sensitive to light. In a couple of years, I would be forced to have a total knee replacement on my left knee just so I could walk. As a result of the fall, I now have three bulging discs in my neck. As a result of the fall, I had severe lower back pain.

In 2012, I lost my job, through which I was making 45k a year. As a result of losing my job, I lost all my health benefits. As a result of losing my health benefits and my job, I had to use all my 401k savings to help pay the mortgage and the bills. After that money was gone, I had to start living off my checking and savings account. After that money was gone, I started to received long term disability from the insurance I had on the job. That money was only enough to pay my mortgage and bills. There were nothing left for pain medication, so I had to start self-medicating myself with Jack Daniel's and pain pills from a drug dealer friend of mine.

Now in 2013, I filed for my Social Security Disability. This was something that the government said I was eligible for due to my age and the years I had worked. However, they denied my claim. I wondered, "God, how much more will you allow me to take? God, are you listening?"

Could Things Get Worse? Yes, They Could.

It was now 2014. I received a letter from Social Security Disability. They have agreed to pay my claim! Finally, some good news after four years of nothing but bad things happening...finally, some good news...or so I thought. After receiving my acceptance letter, I had to forward a copy to the insurance company that was paying my long term disability. I did that and I was shocked by the letter I got back from them. It stated that I had to pay them back all the money that they had paid out to me leading up to the time I get my first check from Social Security Disability. That amount came well over $8,000. That was for six months of back pay.

Later, I got a letter from my long term disability insurance company. The letter stated that if I didn't pay back the money that they paid me prior to getting my Social Security Disability, they would stop my monthly check. God, what else could you allow to happen to me? Just when I thought I had some relief, this was happening. After talking to the insurance company, I was left with no choice but to let the insurance company decrease my monthly payment from $2,100 a month to $859 a month in order to pay back the money that I received from them. I didn't understand why I had to pay it back. I only knew that if I didn't, I was going to lose the rest of my benefit payments.

My Darkest Hours

Now I was thinking about walking away from everything. I was thinking about packing some clothes, getting in my car, and just driving until I ran out of gas. I knew bankruptcy would protect my home and everything I owned, but I was at the end of my rope. When would this end? I was a defeated and beaten down man. I had been through hard times before, but not like this. The loss of a job, health benefits, house in foreclosure, having to file bankruptcy, not being able to drive my car, being behind on bills, and self-medicating with pain pills and alcohol. I thought I could get through it with God's help, but He was nowhere around. There was no help from God and I was out of options. I didn't know what else to do. My Christian upbringing would not let me take my own life or commit suicide, but the thoughts were always there and it seemed like my only option.

I thought about the pain it would cause my mother, my children, sisters, and brothers, but they had no idea of the pain I was suffering through. I was tired of the chronic pain, depression, disappointment, and not being able to sleep. I was tired of having to make choices as to whether I should pay a bill or buy food to eat. At this point, I was just tired of being tired and I just wanted it to end through death or deliverance. I didn't care, whichever one come first.

I thought about all the plans I had for my life and my future. All the things I was going to do. All the trips I was going to take. Now I could barely stand, walk, or drive. My life as I knew it was over. There was no reason to go on living. Because of my injuries, my doctor told me that I would not be able to do a lot of the things that gave me so much joy. The things I did every day and took for granted, like walking, running, dancing, playing basketball, working, or just enjoying a fun day with family and friends.

The chronic pain and depression had taken over my life. Because of it, I no longer wanted to be around family or friends. I tried to tell people what I was going through, but they didn't believe me. No one believes that a fall could cause me so many problems, so I didn't talk about it to any one anymore. There was a time when I participated in life. Now I just sat in the dark and watched it go by. There was a time when life meant something to me. Now it just something I lived every day because I was too afraid to end this so-called existence I called a life.

Facing My Demons

With all the time I had to think about my life, I mostly thought about the past. Having time off work is a great thing, but having time off to think was a bad thing for me. All I did all day and night was to sit and think about the choices I made, the things I did, and what could I have done differently. It was like my own mind was turning against me. I was passing judgment on myself. I don't know if it was caused by the chronic pain I was feeling or the pain pills and alcohol I was taking. All I knew were that the nightmares I had when I went to sleep were terrifying and seemed so real and lifelike. My nightmares would scary Freddy Krueger. Compared to the demons I saw in my nightmares, Jason and Michael Myers looked like saints.

The monsters and the demons that were in my nightmares and in my mind seems very real to me. I

28

have always been a man of the streets and I never feared any man, but what I saw in my mind terrified me to my soul. I would see something that I thought I had gotten over years ago. I dreamed about the things from my past as a little boy. I dreamed about what my dad did to my mom and his kids every night. How he would beat my mom and threatened to kill her and us kids. Every time I closed my eyes, I saw images of my dad and all the bad things he did to my mom his kids. All the beatings and the bad things he did seemed like they were happening in real life every night I went to sleep. The way us kids and my mom had to run for our lives almost daily when he got drunk.

As an adult, I thought the running days were over. I was a grown man in my 50s and I was still running form my dad. He had been dead for ten years! Every time I closed my eyes to sleep at night, I woke up, running for my life. Even though I know it was not real, I would run through my house at night, trying to get away from my dad. Back in the day, I would wake up and find myself running into walls, doors, and over furniture. I broke bones, cut myself, and got other injuries running from my dad in my sleep. Forty years later, he was still chasing me from his grave! I even ran through my bed room window, had to go to the emergency, and had to spend time in the hospital.

My father had been dead for over ten years, but he still chased me every night in my dreams. When I did sleep, I made sure it was only in the day time if I slept at all. In my nightmares, I would see demons eating my eyes and heart. They would tear me apart while I laid there screaming, "God, help me from the pain and terror!" It seemed so real that I would wake up soaking wet with sweat like I just gotten out of the shower.

It got so bad that I gave my friend my gun and told him not to give it back to me. I thought that I was about to use it on myself. I thought I had gotten over that part of my life. I had have spent thousands of dollars over the years on counseling and therapy. Now I prayed that God would hear my plea and take my life either by death of deliverance. I didn't care which one. I was tired of running and I was tired of seeing demons and my dad.

The Pain Worsens; I Weaken

I often think about what my life would have been like if I had had a better male role model in my life. I think about what my life would have been like if I have seen the love that a man should have for his wife or woman. I think about why a man would beat and disrespect the woman that he vowed to love respect and honor - like my dad did. I think about what my life would have been like had I had a functional and loving relationship. I think about what my life would have been like if I could have accepted the love of one woman and not needed to make love to one hundreds. I think about what my life would have been like if my relationships were measured in years and months, not in hours. I think about what my life would have been like if I it didn't let the only woman that I ever loved walk out of my life because I didn't want to change my player lifestyle. I think about what I would have done with my life if I hadn't had four kids by two different women by the age of twenty five. I think about why all the best times and the worst times in my life were spent alone. I wonder if I could have loved just one woman. I think about what might have happened to my life if I had chosen to be the Christian man my mother tried to raise me to be rather than the street man I became. Yes, at that point in my life, I had all the time in the world to ask, "What if?"

Starting My Day with a Jack Daniels Vicodin

Most days, I started my day with a class of Jack Daniel's and two Vicodin. Most of the time, that was the way I ended the days as well. I would only know it was day because I would see a little light coming through the curtains in the living room. I kept the house dark because the bright sun light gave me migraines. I had cut myself off from family and friends. They didn't understand what I was going through.

When I would feel the Vicodin start to work, the pain would lesson. Then, it would be time to do something. I would try to keep up my personal hygiene, which is very hard when you are right-handed and you no longer have the use of your right arm. Things that I did every day and never even thought about, I could no longer do without difficulty because of the pain. These were things like taking a shower, washing my face, brushing my teeth, shaving, or just getting dressed.

I would get so frustrated at God for allowing me to go through this. I wouldn't eat for days because I didn't have the use of my right arm. I couldn't cook. I lived off of Ramen Noodle, Vienna sausage, chips, and TV dinners. When I did go to the store, I would stock up on these things. I stopped buying bottled water because I couldn't twist off the top. I couldn't reach my arm out or hold anything in my right hand. I could stand or walk for only a short period of time because my left knee would give out. I always had the fear that if I would take a shower, my knee would give out and I would fall and hit my head on the tub. The pain coming for my neck, left leg, and knee was even worse than my right shoulder. I had a knee brace on my left leg that I wore every day and night for five years. That was the only way I could walk until 2016, when I had my total knee replacement surgery.

Day and Night: One in the Same

Day and night were the same to me. The only way I could tell the difference was to look at the curtains and see if it was day or night outside. Whenever the pain would worsen, it would be time to take another pill and have a couple more drinks. I'd watch TV all day long, but I didn't understand what was going on. I would doze in and out all day, so it was more like the TV was watching me.

The nightmares were getting worse. I believed the demons would eventually take over my mind and I would do what I needed to do to set myself free from my pain and suffering. The nightmares keep coming at night. When I would try to sleep during the day, sometimes I would see the demons. They talked to me and would tell me that God didn't care about me. If He did, why would He allow me to go through all of this pain and suffering? The demons would ask me why I didn't just put an end to it all so that I would have no more pain and suffering.

I never thought my life would be like this. I didn't know what I did for God to turn His back on me. I had always believed and had faith, but my faith was gone and I had no reason to be believe that things would get better. As I sat there thinking about my past, I believed I had no future. I believed this would be the way my life would end. This was my own private hell, complete with demons and torment. I was thinking that death did not sound so bad. At least the pain would stop. But I had given my gun to a friend and I didn't want to suffer before I died. I was thinking about taking my car and driving it on the highway. When I reached 100 mph, I'd drive it into a bridge.

I had experienced some bad things in my life and I had always pulled through them. I felt for whatever reason that I was alone this time and there would be no divine intervention. I was on my own. I didn't know what else to do. I tried praying, but nothing had happened. My prayers were not being answered. I hated that I had given my gun to my friend, or I would have ended all this that day.

Pastor Linda Willis, AKA "Dude," Saved My Life

One day, as I was sitting home in the dark, I got a call from someone that I never expected to call me. My little sister, "Dude," called me. Dude is what family called her and I had been calling her that since she was a baby. But everybody knew her by the name of Pastor Linda Willis. The call was unexpected - not because we didn't communicate, but because we had always lived two different lifestyles - hers in the church and mine in the streets.

But for the past twenty-five years, she and her husband, Bishop Kevin Willis, were busy building a new church in another city. We didn't have time to talk that much by phone, but we would catch up when they came in town to preach or on holidays. She asked how I was doing. She said I been on her mind a lot lately and that she was working at her desk when a voice told her to stop and call Randy. I told her I was doing well and that everything was great. Then the phone went silent for a few seconds.

"How is the pain you been having?" She asked. "And are you still having those nightmares?" I got quiet for a few seconds. I couldn't say a word. In my mind, I was asking myself how she knew about that. I never told her or anyone about what I was going through. "Randy," she said, "I have to go, but when I am done here, I will call you. We will talk. But before I go, I want to pray for you and tell you one thing." She prayed for me and after she was done, she said, "Randy, God has not turned his back on you. You have turned your back on Him. He is there for you. Just give yourself to Him. Good bye for now. We will talk later."

After she hung up the phone, I just sat there for about five minutes with the phone in my hand. I couldn't believe what I just heard. Later that evening, Dude called again.

"Are you ready to talk?" She asked. "Is now a good time?"

"Yes," I said. But I didn't know how to start. I didn't know what to say after all. This was my baby sister. Sure, we had talked a lot about my lifestyle in the past and she never judge me - but this was different. I had always been able to tell her anything and get advice, but this was very different. I was too ashamed and embarrassed to tell her what I was doing and what I was going through. Somehow, I started talking and it seemed like I talked for hours. When I was done, I heard silence on the phone.

"Hello?" I asked. "Are you there? Did you listen to

anything I said?"

"Yes, I am here," she said, "And I heard every word you said. While you were talking, I was on my knees, praying for you. I had the phone on speaker phone. I heard every word. Randy, God has revealed to me that the devil is after your mind and soul. What you have to do is trust in Him and rely on your Christian upbringing. You may have strayed away from the path, but God is there for you to lead you down the right road. I have to go now. We will talk tomorrow. God has always been there for you. All you have to do is reach out to Him."

I was sitting and thinking about our conversation. Then the phone rang. It was Dude on the other end.

"Good morning," she said.

"Morning," I said. "We just talked a little while ago."

"Boy," she laughed, "That was over ten hours ago!" I had sat there all night thinking about what she had said and I didn't even know it! She told me that overnight, "God laid something in my spirit for me to tell you."

"There is help for you close by," she said. When I asked where, she replied, "I don't know, but trust Him and believe what He says."

Writing the Pain Hurt and Anger Away

One day, as Dude and I were talking, she asked me if I was still having trouble falling asleep at night.

35

"Yes," I said, "I can't sleep because my thoughts are racing in my mind."

"Why don't you try putting your thoughts on paper? I suggest that to a lot of people I counsel, and it helps them," she advised. "Didn't you say that when you retired, you wanted to write your memoirs? The story of your life? You don't have to write every day - only the times when you can't sleep."

"That will be every day," I said. We both laughed.

"I will call you in a couple of days to check on you and see how everything is going," she said. "Let's pray now." After we were done, she said, "Randy, trust and believe in God because He still believes in you."

After she hung up the phone, I got out my laptop and tried to write, but I couldn't think of anything to write about. I did not think this was for me. Later that night as I lay in my bed, looking into the darkness, my thoughts started to race in my mind. I got up, went to the living room, and started to write. It was about 12:30 a.m. As my thoughts raced through my mind, I put them down on paper. Then the phone rang! It was my mom.

"Mom!" I said. "Is everything alright? Why are you call me? It's 12:30 in the morning!"

"Boy," she said, "Look at your clock. It's 9:00 in the morning." I couldn't believe it! I had been up all night writing. "I was just checking on you. Do you need anything? Is everything alright?"

"No," I said, "I don't need anything. Everything is

alright now." As I stopped to read what I had written, I realized that I had written nineteen pages about my young life. I felt some of the pain and anger starting to leave. I did something that I haven't done in four years. I laid down and took a nap.

Writing became a way for me to channel my hurt, fear, anger, and frustration, I would start writing about 12 - 1 a.m. and write all night until 9 -10 a.m. Then I would take a much needed break, a cat nap. Through this process, I was able to clear my mind. Much like you would with your e-mail, I would write about something, then deleted it from my mind. By doing this, I was able to write my life story and several other books that I eventually had published. Thank you, Pastor Linda Willis, AKA "Dude." You saved my life!

Pastor Linda Willis Fixed My Mind; Now It's Time to fix My Body

The year was 2015. One day, I was out running some errands. I heard a commercial about a Pain Management Clinic. It was five minutes from my house! I wrote down the number, called, and told them my story just to see if they could help me. They made me an appointment for me for the next day to come in and see the doctor.

I explained to the doctor that my work compensation had ended two years beforehand. After examining me and looking at the MRI of all my injuries, he said he would reopen my case. Additionally, he put me in a pain management program so I could get the help physically and mentally that I needed. That's sounded great to me. After two years, I was finally going to get some help.

37

"Randy," the doctor asked me, "With these types of injuries, how were you able to deal with all that pain?" I was too embarrassed and ashamed to tell him that I had been self-medicating with alcohol and with pain pills. I said I been taking Advil and Tylenol. The doctor looked at me and gave me that look like he knew I was lying.

In the Pain Management Program, I got the help I needed. I was finally getting therapy and legal pain medication. I had to have a second rotator cuff surgery that year, but I had help from professionals, therapy, support, and pain management. Thank you, God, my father. You brought me through my darkest hour.

Reconnection with God

Now that my mind and body was being fixed, it was time to repair my spirit and my relationship with God. I call Dude and asked her what how to start. She told me to start and end every day with a prayer.

"Every week," she said, "I will give you some scriptures to read. At the end of every week, I will call you and we will talk about them." So that Sunday night, she give five scriptures and said she would call me at the end of the week to see how I was doing. "There will be a test when I call!" She added.

That week, I read and studied all five scriptures and made notes. On Friday, I was very nervous. I didn't know if I was going to get this right. At 7:30 p.m., Dude called.

""Hello?" I said.

"Hello and how are you doing?" She asked. "Did you complete your assignment?" I told her I did. She said, "Let me hear them." I went down the list one scripture at a time. As I read them, I told her what I got from each scripture.

"How did I do?" I asked when I was finished. I was very nervous about what she had to say. "Did I pass?" I asked. She laughed.

"Boy," she said, "There are no right or wrong answers. Everybody gets something different from those scriptures. This is my way of letting you find out what you need for you. Randy, God told me to start you on your path, but that He would lead you down that path. This was just my way to get you started. You have a long journey ahead of you and I am here anytime you need me." With that said, we prayed together and she gave me five more scriptures to read.

As the weeks passed, we would discuss each scripture. "Randy," she would say, :God wants you to do more than just believe in Him. He wants you to serve Him in His church. He wants you to help and support His church by paying your offering and tithes. God said, 'As you sow, you will reap.' I don't expect for you to understanding these things now. But as you grow in the word and follow God's teachings, He will reveal these things to you."

Dude was right. As the months went by and as I grew in the word and did as God asked, I began to see a change in my life, health, and finances. The things that kept me up all night long, I no longer thought about anymore. I am proud to say that after over thirty years of running from my dad and bad nightmares, I finally got my first eight hours of sleep on August 29, 2015. Thank you, Dude, AKA Pastor Linda Willis. I give all the praise to God, my father.

God Saved a Life Across the Country Through Me

This is a story that I never told anyone, not even Dude. Sometimes, I don't believe it happened myself, but it did happen. I don't know why it happened or how it happened, but it did. Now I want to share it with my readers.

One night, as I was doing some research on the Internet for one of my books, I found myself in a chat room. Now other than words, this was the extent of my knowledge about the Internet. So I found myself filling out a profile.

The next day, I received a friend request from a lady. Let's call her Doris. She lived in Sacramento, California. She said she read my profile. She was also a Cowboys fan, even though they'd had a few bad years. We had a few more things in common. She was retried too and we were both Scorpios. It was getting late and I was tired of chatting.

"Doris," I asked, "Do you want to exchange numbers and pick up this conversation tomorrow?" She said yes and we did. I thought that I would never get to meet her, as she lived so far away. Talking on the phone was cool. I wasn't doing anything else during the day but studying scriptures and working on my book.

After we hung up the phone, I continued to work on my book. For some reason, Doris was on my mind. The next morning, I got up and was working on my book, when a voice came to me and said, "Call Doris." I ask myself why, when I heard the voice again, "Call Doris." I said to myself that there was a two hour time difference between California and Dallas. It was 6:00 a.m. here and 4:00 a.m. there. I was not calling anyone at 4:00 a.m. in the morning.

Just then, my phone ring. It was Doris on the other line!

"Good morning," she said. "I hope I didn't wake you. I know it's about 6:00 a.m. there.

"No," I said, "I was just doing some writing. What's on your mind?" As she started to tell me what was going on in her life, I came to find out we had identical stories - except her injuries occurred from an automobile accident. As she talked and I heard her crying, I started to relive the last five years of my life.

"Thank you, Randy," she said, "For listening. No one else cares - not family or friends."

"Doris," I said, "I know what you are going through. I went through that same thing for four years." I started to tell her my story. It seemed like I talked to her for hours.

"Randy," she said when I finished, "I will call you tomorrow and we will pick up where we left off." I agreed. The next day, I called Doris. No answer. I tried to call her for a couple of weeks without any luck. I through to myself that if she wants to talk, she would call me.

Over a year went by. One day, I was on the

Internet on a chat site. There was a message from Doris with a number. "Call me, Randy, when you can." It was a different number, so I called and she answered.

"Doris?" I asked.

"Yes, who is this?" She asked.

"Randy from Dallas," I said. Then I heard a lot of crying and screaming. I think she dropped the phone. I heard a loud crash.

"Are you there?" She asked.

"Yes," I said, "Are you okay?"

"Yes," she replied. "Randy, when I heard your voice, I started to shout and pray." Now I was thinking that I had made women do a lot of things, but shouting and praying has never been one of them. As she started to talk to me, I couldn't believe what she was saying. "Randy, you saved my life." Now I was confused. I didn't even know this lady that well and we had never met. She was telling me I saved her life? I thought this woman was crazy. "Randy, do you remember the day you and I talked? After our conversation, I was going to go across the street to the park, smoke a cigarette, and blow my brains out of my head. But your testimony about what God had done for you changed that."

"What?" I asked. "What did I say?"

"Randy, your story about what you went through was the same thing I was going through. But I was using crack and cocaine to deal with my problems. After listening to your story, you made me laugh. You made me cry! But you made me find Jesus. Like you, Randy, I was raised in a Christian house with a Christian upbringing. My father was a preacher. After my accident, my world collapsed, just like yours. The day before you and I talked, I went and had all the utilities cut off in my home. I left my family a note telling them why I did what I did. But after listening to you witness to me about how God brought you through, I went to that park, laid my gun on the grass, and I begin to pray. As I was praying, a man walked up to me and began to pray next to me. Someone saw the gun and called the police. They came they kept the gun. After seeing I was alright, they let me go. Randy, to make a long story short, the man that was praying for me was a preacher. He told me that God told him to go to that park because someone needed him. Now, Randy, he and I are married. We have our own outreach ministry program. We are helping people who suffer from drugs, alcohol, and depression problems."

I couldn't say anything. I just stood there, lifeless. I couldn't believe something that I said to a stranger would save a life. I have always heard God works in mysterious ways, and He work though me to save a life across the country.

God Tore Me Down To Build Me Up

I was in a pain management program. I was getting some much needed help. Even though my body was being fixed, my spirit and soul was badly in need of repair.

One morning, as I was writing, I thought I heard

43

someone say something to me. I stopped and looked around. There wasn't anyone in the house but me and the dogs. They were in the bedroom, asleep under the bed. As a continued to write, I heard a voice.

"Give your life to me." I felt a chill and I stopped typing. I fell to my knees.

"Take me, Lord! I am yours!" I must have prayed and shouted so loudly that I woke up and scared the dogs. At that moment, I knew that God had a purpose for my life. But I knew He had to test my faith in Him before He would reveal what it was. I had to prove myself worthy of Him before He would reveal what that purpose was. Like Pastor Linda Willis told me, God never turned His back on me. I turned my back on Him. He never lost faith in me, even though I lost my faith in Him.

Now five years later, my body and mind had been healed and I had a great life. I found my way back. I have been blessed in ways that I could never imagine. I always joke with "Dude" Pastor Linda Willis by saying that I have felt God's wrath, and now I am receiving His blessing. We both laugh at this. I realize now that God had to completely tear the man I was down to build me into the man He wanted me to be. All the things I went through were His way of telling me that when He was done with me, I would be a better man - the man He wanted me to be.

Thank you, God, my father. Now, I must confess that I am not that man yet, but I work on him every day. With God having my back, I know I will be that man very soon. I understand you can't take a mess that took 58 years create and fix it overnight. I realize my journey has just begun and I have a long way to go. But God has put some good people in my path to help me, like Bishop Kevin Willis, Pastor Linda Willis, and my mom. They help me and keep me strong.

Doing Better Than Ever

The year was 2016 and life was good. I finally had that knee surgery I needed for my left knee. I had to have a total knee replacement surgery from the accident I had from the fall in 2011. I was focused on the rehabilitation of my knee and building my relationship with God, thanks to Dude, AKA Pastor Linda Willis' life- saving advice to me to write my thought down on paper.

I wrote and published my books in 2016. All these books can be found on Amazon.com, Barnes and Noble.com, and my website, randywallacebooks.com.

In 2016, God blessed me with a large insurance settlement that I been waiting on for years from that same insurance company that made me pay back all that money. Well, after doing the things you would normally do when you come into some extra money, I blessed my church, New Life in Christ Church, and my Mom's church, Greater Mount Sinai Baptist Church. I paid off a lot of bills, bought some new clothes, replaced old furniture, and fixed up some things around the house. I blessed my family.

After doing all of these things, I asked God about the money left for myself.

"So, what do you want me to do with the rest?"

"Randy," God spoke to me, "I want you to bless twenty-five people with no less than a hundred dollars each."

So the next morning, I went to the bank and took out the money. I started blessing people. For weeks, I blessed people. Some people I knew, and some people I didn't know. I was surprised to see the joy that the money brought to those people. Some people cried and some people gave me the praise. I told them to give all the praise to God. I was just doing what I was told to do.

Now, I am living large off less. God takes care of my needs and helps to get the things I want. God is good.

Reflecting on my Christian Childhood Upbringing

Now, at night, I sit and think about all those times my mother would march us to church every Sunday. As a little boy, my mother was over what I thought at the time every auxiliary in the church. Man, we went to Sunday School at 9:00 a.m. in the morning, then 11:00 a.m. services. If there was a 3:00 p.m. program, we were there. We attended Sunday evening services at 6:00 p.m. for BTU (Baptist Training Union), choir practice on Tuesday, and Bible Study on Wednesday Bible. At Christmas, we were in the Christmas play. At Easter, we had a speech to say. If there was a play, we were in it, too. During summer time, we went to Vacation Bible School. She churched us for what I thought was ever.

To this day, over frothy five years later, I can still recite all the books of the Bible in the Old Testament and most of them in the New Testament. I still remember the game we would play in BTU. An adult would call out a scripture from the Bible and we would race to find it. Whoever found it first stood up and read it. If you were first, you won a prize. I never won anything. I still know the words to that old song that went like this: "Give me that BTU sprit!"

It was good enough for my mother and it is good enough for me. My mother taught her children a lot about God and the Bible - at church and at home. Even though I did stray away from the path of the church, I never forgot my mother's teachings and the church.

My God is a Mighty God

It is now July, 2017. I have completed all the requirements and conditions of my bankruptcy. All my credit debt has been dismissed or has been charged off. I now have a new start at life. With this new start comes a 680 credit score from completing the program and a mortgage modification that reduced my mortgage payment by $650 a month. By being declared disabled to work by Social Security, the taxes on my home were reduced from $3,191 a year to $191 a year.

As I sat reading the letter, I thought about an old song that we children would sing in BTU that went like this:. "Amazing Grace, how sweet the sound that saved a wretch like me. I once was lost, but now am found. I was blind, but now I see."

I serve and pray to a mighty God, one who is forgiving, loving, and merciful. A God who asks only that you serve Him, honor Him, and trust and believe in

Him. Even after He has taken away all the things you thought were so important in your life. For doing these things, He rewards you with things that are a hundred times more and better than you ever had. He did it for me. Yes, I serve a mighty God. Sometimes I sit and think that if not for my God, I don't know how I would have gotten over my trials.

A Tribute to my Mom

On September 13, 2017, God call my mother home to be with Him, but He did allow me to spend 58 of the best years of my life with this remarkable woman. She was always Mom to me, but she was so much more to her own family and church family. As a Sunday school and B.T.U. (Baptist Training Union) teacher, she taught all the children in the church, including my siblings and me, about the Bible and God's word. She served her church faithfully as President of the Mission Board for over thirty years.

One day, as a little boy, I saw my mom sitting at the table, reading her Bible.

"Mom," I asked her, "How can you believe in God when you can't see Him?" She picked me up and set me down on her knee.

"Randy," she said, "Do you believe in Christmas?"

"Yes," I said.

"Can you see Christmas?"

"No," I said.

"But you believe it is coming?"

"Yes," I replied.

"That's the way my God works," Mom said. "I can't see Him, but I know and believe He is always there."

It took me forty years to figure that one out. My mom had a lot of battles in her life, just like everyone else. One of her greatest battles was with cancer. But her faith, strong belief in God, and determination always pulled her though. In July, 2017, at the age of 83, she became a three time cancer survivor. She never let cancer stop her from doing the things she most liked to do in life, such as attending church, shopping, and getting her hair and nails done - in that order!

People that know her always said, "If you want to find her, look in one of these three places: Greater Mt. Sinai Baptist Church, the Galleria Mall, North Park Mall, or the nail salon, in that order."

Even though cancer had taken over her body, she always said that God had her spirit. I believe He did, because in 2016, my mom did something that she had never done before at the age of 83. She brought home a new Honda Accord! You may wonder what's so special about that. All of her family and church family knew mom, also known as Sister People, got a new Honda Accord every two years. It was always the same color - Charcoal Gray. But this year, she surprised everybody and got a dark brown car! That's when everybody start asking if she was alright. We all thought she had lost her mind. We asked her why, after twenty years, she changed the color of her car.

"That's my prerogative," she answered to people. "I can do what I want to do."

"Go on, Sister People!" We cheered.

Mom, I know you knew this, but I need to say it. I

love you so much and miss you every day. I may not have been the best child you had, but you were the best mom any boy could ever want. I love you, mom.

Should I or Shouldn't I Write This?

Now it's 2017. My mind is healed, my body is healed, and God is still working on my spirit. I am in a much better place now than I have ever been in my life. I want to share my story with others - my testimony on what God has done for me and how he delivered me. I went from a man who needed pain pills and alcohol just to start and end his day to a man who talks to God every day and put Him first in everything he does. I wanted to tell the world what God has done for me and to me, but I was ashamed of what people might think or say. So I did what I normally do when I had a problem - I called "Dude," AKA Pastor Linda Willis. As we talked, I told her about the book idea and that I was struggling with the decision as to whether I should or shouldn't write it.

"Boy! I have read your other books," Dude said, "And you were not ashamed to tell the world those stories about your life. But you are ashamed to tell the world how God helped you heal and saved your life? Randy, God said that if you are ashamed of Him, He will be ashamed of you. So do what God is telling you to do."

So that night, before going to bed, I had a talk with God. Now, you are reading my story. I have always said that there were only three things I wanted out of life: own my own home find that special lady to spend the rest of my life with, and give my life to God and do His work. At this point, I do own my own home, I may not find that special woman at 58, and my dedication to God is a work in progress. But you know, two out of three is not bad.

New Life in Christ; New Outlook on Life

I'm living my new life in Christ's Church and am a member of New Life Church, led by Bishop Kevin Willis and Pastor Linda Willis. I am happy that I finally got to see you and meet some of your members. After seven years of watching you online, I finally went to the church and met the people. I am what you may call a Media Member. I see you every Sunday online. I watched you grow from a church that had less than fifty members and one Sunday service to a church that has two services every Sunday and over a thousand members. Even though I am not in New Life Church on Sunday physically, my spirit is there with you every week. So keep up the good work; you are changing lives. Bishop Kevin Willis and Pastor Linda Willis and all the New Life family - be blessed and keep changing lives. Special thanks to my nephew, Quincy Preston, for all the help you gave me with my books. Be blessed, all of you. I thank you all. You are truly transforming lives to save the world. You transformed my life and saved me.

My Inspirational Thoughts to Others

I would like to say a few things to anyone reading my book. No matter what you are going through, lean on God and His strength and guidance in your Darkest Hour. He will be there for you. I know you might think there is no why out of your situation or problem. All you need to do is give the problems to God. There is no situation for which He can't find an solution. There is no problem He can't solve. All things are possible if you believe. Please get some professional help from your Bishop, Pastor, Preacher, Minister, or family. Please don't try to go at it alone. Some things are just bigger than you are and you need help with them.

Remember, God tests our faith in many different ways. This might be His test for you. I hope and pray that whatever you are going through, you will know God will bring you through it. Don't turn your back on Him because He will never turn his back on you. I thank you for reading my book and keeping me in your prayers. Be blessed. Keep your faith and trust in God no matter what. I did, and look where He has brought me!

Giving Praise and Special Thanks to God

I would like to give praise to God for bringing me though all the madness that was my life. I know if it wasn't for His mercy, grace, favor, and forgiveness, I would not be here today. I could have ended up in prison, taken my own life, or died from HIV or AIDS because of the lifestyle I was living.

Very Special Thanks to My Mother

I would like to give a very special thanks to my mother, whom I love so much. I know back in the day I kept you on your knees, praying to God to look over me and keep me safe as I was out in the world doing things I had no business doing. I know you have always been a woman of God and you always had a special relationship with Him. You always had His ear. I bet sometimes, when you would pray to God, He would look down on you and say, "Oh, no! Not Randy, again!"

53

I love you, Mom.

Thank you, Bishop Kevin and Pastor Linda Willis

Thank you for all of your years of support and the love you have shown me. You knew my lifestyle, but you never judged me. I was always welcome in your home and your church. Thank you, both. I love you both.

Special Thanks to "Dude," AKA Pastor Linda Willis

Thank you! Over the years, you have been my Pastor, Psychologist , Spiritual Advisor, Life Coach, Counselor, and a sympathetic ear when I needed one. I needed all of those things. The best part is that you never charged me a thing! Thank you. I love you, Dude.

To My Family and Friends: Thank You

Thank you to everyone who has told me, "Boy! You need to get some Jesus in your life." I know and I did. Next, thanks to that little, old-school, church-going sister who lived under me in the apartments. She would see me running different women in and out of my apartment, day and night.

"Son, I'm praying for you," she would say as she stood there with her arm crossed, shaking her head. Thank you all. I love you and be blessed.

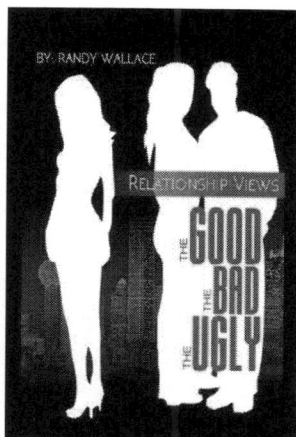

CHECK OUT THESE OTHERS TITLES
BY RANDY WALLACE

ALL TITLES AVAILABLE ON

Made in the USA
Lexington, KY
06 February 2018